FAST FROM WRONG THINKING

A 40-DAY
Journey to Change
from the Inside Out

GREGORY DICKOW

Fast from Wrong Thinking

A 40-Day Journey to Change from The Inside Out

©2016 by Gregory Dickow Ministries.

All rights reserved.

No part of this book may be used or reproduced in any manner whatsoever—graphic, electronic, or mechanical—without written permission, except in the case of reprints in the context of reviews.Scripture quotations marked (AMP) are taken from the Amplified Bible, Copyright © 1954, 1958, 1962, 1964, 1965, 1987

by The Lockman Foundation. Used by permission.

Printed in the United States of America

For information, please write

*Gregory Dickow Ministries
PO Box 7000
Chicago, IL 60680*

or visit us online at *www.gregorydickow.org.*

First printing, 2016

Table of Contents

What Others Are Saying 5
Introduction 11
Day 1: I Feel Powerless 13
Day 2: I Feel like Giving Up 16
Day 3: I Can't 18
Day 4: It's Too Late 20
Day 5: I Am Afraid 23
Day 6: I Feel So Angry 26
Day 7: I'm Overwhelmed 29
Day 8: God Is Mad at Me 31
Day 9: I Don't Have Enough 34
Day 10: God Is Far from Me 37
Day 11: My Life Is out of Control 40
Day 12: I Can't Seem to Stop This Anxiety 43
Day 13: I Just Can't See Things Getting Better 45
Day 14: It's Impossible 47
Day 15: I Feel Guilty 50
Day 16: It's Just So Hard to Be a Christian 53
Day 17: The Future Is Fearful and Uncertain 55
Day 18: Something Bad Is Going to Happen to Me
or My Family. 58

Day 19: How Could Something So Bad Ever Turn Into Something Good 61
Day 20: It's Too Hard to Find God's Will 63
Day 21: I Just Can't Forgive Myself 65
Day 22: I'm Inferior 68
Day 23: Happiness Is So Hard to Find 70
Day 24: It's Hopeless 72
Day 25: I'm Offended 74
Day 26: I Can't Stop 76
Day 27: I Haven't Done Enough to Get God to Answer My Prayers or Bless Me 78
Day 28: I Don't Feel Loved 80
Day 29: I Don't Think This Pain Will Ever Go Away 83
Day 30: My Life Is Not as Good as Others'. 85
Day 31: I'm Stuck 88
Day 32: This Problem Is Too Big 91
Day 33: I Can't Shake My Past 93
Day 34: I Feel Cursed 95
Day 35: I'll Never Be Able to Change This Area of My Life . . 97
Day 36: Fasting from Excuses 99
Day 37: Fasting from Small Thinking 102
Day 38: I'm Stressed Out 105
Day 39: I Feel like I've Failed 107
Day 40: I'm Limited 109
Conclusion 112

What Others Are Saying

"**The testimony of Jesus is the spirit of prophecy.**" **Revelation 19:10.**

We constantly receive miraculous testimonies from people who have experienced firsthand the power of fasting from wrong thinking. Here are just a few of them. Let their stories serve as a prophecy, or prediction, of the great things that you can expect to happen in your life. Get ready for *your* revolution—from the inside out!

—Gregory Dickow

50-year addiction broken—

I recently completed your 40-day Fast from Wrong Thinking. As a result, I quit smoking shortly after! I had smoked for over 50 years of my life, now I've been four months clean, with no craving at all! Only God! Thank you, Pastor Dickow, for being real, and doing all that God has planned for you, according to His will. Amen!
—Debrah

No longer suicidal—

I've been getting your 40 thoughts to fast from, and it has changed my life. I started listening to you while channel surfing after being away from

God for nine years, but I don't believe it was an accident. You were teaching on being free from fear. I had been *so* scared of Isis and a potential war that I was planning my own suicide. Jesus came on the scene through your teaching and set me free from anxiety, fear, and depression. I am free. God bless you! **—Evelyn**

Marriage restored—

I began to receive the 40-day Fast from Wrong Thinking during a very bad time in my marriage. My wife moved out, and I realized she wasn't coming back. About 20 days into the Fast from Wrong Thinking, I angrily told her to get out of the house. Four days passed, and I realized that she wasn't coming back. She said the pain she felt was too much. On day 38 of the Fast from Wrong Thinking, it still looked hopeless.

But on day 39, I read your message and began to expect the tables to turn. At noon, my wife came home! Something had happened in her heart, and she felt she could give me this one last chance for our family. The Lord restored my family back, and I know I'm a different man now! **—James**

Son changed in prison—

My 19-year-old son had been incarcerated; and while in prison, I had been sending him copies of the Fast from

Wrong Thinking. As a result, he rededicated his life to the Lord, and he began ministering to others and leading them to Christ—right in the prison! He and the other inmates love the Fast from Wrong Thinking. Within two weeks, he was released from prison, and the charges were miraculously dropped! **—Christine**

Freed from anxiety, depression, and fear—

Dear Pastor, I live in the Netherlands and have been doing the Fast from Wrong Thinking for a year, and I now have total victory in my life! I had been fighting depression for 14 years. I could never think straight and had worries all the time—anxiety and fear. For two years, I had been looking for a job, while applying every week with two or more applications. But little by little, all this was going away with every thought you sent. Today I praise God because I have a new job that is exactly what I had asked the Lord for.

In a Sunday church service (online), when you prayed for those looking for a job, you said in 30 days they have a job. The next day, I was hired on my new job. God bless your ministry greatly! Now I can think clearly, I am free, and I have peace in my mind and in my spirit. I feel at peace with God and loved by Him! **—Vlad**

Freed from anger—

Dear Pastor, I have noticed a wonderful change in my everyday life. My thinking is changing, and my actions are following. I have noticed how I handled a situation with my husband. Anger did not control me. Neither did emotional bashing of myself. I am accepting that I have rights, because Jesus gave me these rights. There have been times when the old thinking tries to come into play, but I find myself trying to remember what thought should I replace it with. The thought on Day 27 was especially meaningful to me, and when I read it for the first time, it touched me deep inside. I felt like I wanted to cry. I have confidence now over that negative thought that has plagued me my whole adult life. Thank you! **—Marie**

Healed of PTSD—

I praise God that you were obedient to God to start the Fast from Wrong Thinking. I don't want to know, nor will I think of where my life would be without going through it. I never stopped this life-changing fast and was healed of a lifetime of Post Traumatic Stress Disorder! If you've never had it, you don't want to know what that's like. I praise God daily for my healing. Thank you again! **—Vicky**

Freed from fear—

Over 10 years ago, my ex-boyfriend tried to kill me. He sliced my throat, stabbed me multiple times, and left me in a ditch for dead. For years I have lived in fear of what he would do if he finds me when released from prison. Six days into the Fast from Wrong Thinking, the feeling of fear has left me completely! I know now, more than ever, that I serve a God bigger than any abuse I have ever faced. I look forward to the testimonies to come over the next 40 days! —**Charlotte**

Free from 31-year addiction—

Pastor Dickow, I have gotten so much from your Fasting from Wrong Thinking. I am learning to apply *His Word* to my everyday life. I have never felt so free in my entire life. I am now free from a 31-year addiction, and it's only the grace of God that I'm alive to share this with you. Before this year, I knew Jesus, but not personally. Now I know God is faithful, and I am going to succeed in making something good out of all the bad. —**Betsy**

Lost 11 pounds—

I started the Fast from Wrong Thinking and I lost 11 pounds without even trying! I didn't even have the desire for eating as much when I started changing the way I thought. During that time, I went to my doctor for a check up and he was so surprised, he asked me, "What diet are you on?" I looked at him and said, "Diet nothing! I went on a Fast from Wrong Thinking with Gregory Dickow! —**Amber**

Healed from Insomnia—

You need to know that during the last 40-day Fast from Wrong Thinking, I was completely healed from insomnia after many years. I can finally sleep through the night. I wake up refreshed and renewed! Fasting from wrong thinking has changed everything. —**Samuel**

Patients healed—

I am a Christian counselor. Our ministry works with marriages and individuals in crisis, and your Fast from Wrong Thinking has been a great tool that God has used to help bring His truth and His healing to our clients. It is amazing how often our clients would need the exact word God had given you for that day. God has ministered greatly to me as an individual believer, as well as my clients, through this fast. Thank you for being willing to be such an effective conduit for God's truth and power to flow through.—**Jerry**

Introduction
Changed: From the Inside Out

We are about to go on an unprecedented journey, which carries with it the remarkable DNA of change!

A number of years ago, I was frustrated when I saw so many people desiring change in their lives, but failing to see results. Out of this frustration, I believe God spoke to me and said, "Call My people to **fast from wrong thinking**." In that moment, a movement was born, which has powerfully impacted hundreds of thousands of people around the world. It's NOT a fast from food, but a fast from wrong mind-sets and thoughts that keep us limited and defeated.

Just as a butterfly is designed by God to fly, so are you! However, the butterfly can only emerge in its beautiful color and magnificent wings after it has been transformed within the warm cocoon of its Creator. What starts as a caterpillar is miraculously transformed into one of the most beautiful creatures God has ever made.

This Fast from Wrong Thinking devotional is your cocoon. As you wrap your mind in God's thoughts over the next 40 days, you too will be miraculously transformed, and you will *begin to fly!*

This is exactly the miraculous metamorphosis that God describes in Romans 12:2, when He says, *"Be transformed by the renewing of your mind."* That's what fasting from wrong thinking is all about. The Message Bible tells us that as you do this, *"You'll be changed from the inside out."*

The way we think controls our entire life. Our thoughts shape our words, actions, and habits. Our thoughts release God's potential in our lives or limit us from experiencing His best. The Bible says it best:

"For as a man thinks within, so is he . . . " (Proverbs 23:7)

Jesus said to take His yoke, because it's easy and His burden is light (Matthew 11:30). That's the grace of God. He did the heavy lifting, and now, our job is to enter into His rest. This is accomplished when you begin to believe what God has already provided. That's what this journey is all about. It will awaken you to His work of GRACE in your life! You will be amazed at just how easy this will be.

It's time for you to take control of your life by taking control of your thoughts. It's time to stop living below your privileges and rights as a child of God.

I can tell you from my own experience and the amazing testimonies of others that what follows on these pages will be the catalyst for a life beyond your greatest dreams. Are you ready to eliminate the mind-sets that have limited and confined you? Ready to awaken the unlimited possibilities of God?

Then let's go!

Gregory Dickow

DAY 1
"I Feel Powerless."

One of the greatest truths I have ever come to understand is that a *sense of powerlessness* is the root to all negative emotions. When we feel powerless over our past, we feel guilty. When we feel powerless over our future, we feel afraid. When we feel powerless over the present, we feel depressed. And when we feel like the people or circumstances of our lives just won't change, we feel angry.

Think about this for a moment—depression, fear, guilt and anger are four of the most powerful negative emotions you will ever experience, and all of them stem from a sense of powerlessness. The thought that there's not much we can do about the economy, or our weight, or the allergies we grew up with forces us to accept and tolerate a mediocre and weak life.

As we begin this 40-day journey today, lets fast from the thought that says, **"I feel powerless."**

LET'S CHANGE IT TODAY

1. **Take inventory!** God has not given you a spirit of fear; but power, love, and a sound mind (2 Timothy 1:7).

2. **Believe that power is in you.** Ephesians 3:20 says, God is able to do exceeding abundantly above all we can ask or think according to the power that is at work within you. There is power in you that enables God to do beyond what you can ask or think!

3. **THINK AND ASK BIG.** Give God something to work with. Because He can do beyond, we have to at least give Him a base to begin with. We limit God when we don't think big and ask big.

4. **Recognize and honor the Holy Spirit in you.** Acts 1:8 says, "You shall receive power when the Holy Spirit comes upon you . . ." This power (*dunamis* is the Greek word for dynamite) is already in you. Thank God for the Holy Spirit in you. Romans 8:11 says, "The very same Spirit that raised Jesus from the dead lives in you."

5. **Take the limits off.** Don't limit God. Psalm 78:41 says that the children of Israel limited the Lord because they did not remember His power (verse 42). We free God's Hand to bless when we remember His previous blessings. Psalm 103:2 says to remember His blessings.

6. **EXPECT!** Never underestimate the power of expectation. Expect God's power to strengthen

you today. Expect to be led by His Spirit. We limit what God can do in our lives when we lower our expectations.

7. **Embrace your power.** You have the power to forgive and be forgiven (John 20:23); the power to heal (Mark 16:20); the power to speak the Word and see results (Job 22:28).

THINK IT AND SAY IT

I have **POWER** in my life right now. Through the Holy Spirit in me, I have the power to overcome temptation, the power to change my life for the better, the power to be healed, the power to forgive and the power to speak God's Word and see His promises show up in my life.

I will think big and ask big, and therefore the **POWER OF GOD'S SPIRIT WITHIN ME** will bring it to pass in my life, in Jesus' Name!

Day 2

"I Feel like Giving Up."

Today we are fasting from the thought that says, **"I feel like giving up."**

We might feel like giving up on anything from our faith, to our marriage, to life itself. Why do we sometimes feel like giving up? Because of the way we think.

LET'S CHANGE IT TODAY

1. **God never gives up on you.** (Hebrews 13:5) "I will not [I will not; I will not] ever leave you or forsake you . . ." He doesn't give up on you, and He has put His spirit of perseverance in you.

2. **You have power. God has given you POWER!** (2 Timothy 1:7) You have the power to endure.

3. **Get to the root.** Fear and anxiety make people faint and quit. Luke 21:26 says, ". . . men's hearts fainting from fear, and for the anxious expectation of what is coming on the world." Ask God for a revelation of His perfect love for you. Fear will leave (1 John 4:18).

4. **Your thoughts control your feelings.** Don't worry about the feelings. Deal with the thoughts. Your feelings will follow.

5. **It's just your imagination.** *Giving up* starts in your thinking (Hebrews 12:3) and then becomes an imagination, which then leads to a stronghold. (2 Corinthians 10:3–5) Speak to these thoughts, and they will obey you.

6. **Remember: He is your Finisher.** Hebrews 12:2 says, "He is the author and finisher of your faith." Whatever you feel you can't finish—Jesus will finish for you, in you, and through you. Fix your eyes on Him. Fix your mind and eyes on Jesus right now.

THINK IT AND SAY IT

I will not be moved by the feelings of giving up. God doesn't quit on me, so I won't quit. I have the power to persevere. I am made in God's image. Fear makes people quit, and God's perfect love for me drives out fear.

I speak to the thoughts of giving up, and I command them to leave my life. Jesus is the author and finisher of my faith, so I cannot fail, in Jesus' Name!

(Pg 53) Putting The word of God...

Day 3

"I Can't..."

As we continue this fast from wrong thinking, remember: *Fasting* is not limited to food. It's about *abstaining* from something. In our case, we are abstaining, or "fasting" from wrong ways of thinking.

Today we are fasting from the thought that says, **"I can't."**

There's a saying that goes, "If you think you can or you think you CAN'T, you're right." Either way, you're right, because as a man thinks, so is he (Proverbs 23:7).

Every day we are troubled or even tormented by thoughts that say: "I can't change. I can't go on. I can't make it. I can't forgive. I can't recover. I can't get it done. I can't find a job. I can't find a spouse. I can't pay the bills." And the list could go on and on.

The Spirit of God lives on the inside of you. That means you CAN do what He can do in you. 1 John 4:17 says, "As He is, so are we in this world."

LET'S CHANGE IT TODAY

1. **Remember the little engine that could!** Remember the book that spoke to a generation of children: "I think I can. I think I can. I think I can," AND IT DID!

2. **Say it: "I can."** By simply saying this continually, your life will take the turn you desire.

3. **You ARE, therefore you CAN.** Remember that you ARE already more than a conqueror; therefore you CAN conquer anything (Romans 8:37).

4. **BELIEVE the Bible is written about YOU.** Fill your mind with Philippians 4:13: "I CAN DO ALL things through Christ which strengthens me!"

5. **Changing your thinking will change your habits.** Stop yourself every time you feel like saying "I can't"; and let this new thought "I can" come out of your mouth. The more your ears hear your voice say this, the easier it becomes to believe it.

THINK IT AND SAY IT

I declare I can do all things through Jesus Christ who strengthens me. I eliminate "can't" from my vocabulary. I can do anything God's Word says I can do. I submit my thinking to the Word of God and my whole life is changing today, in Jesus' Name!

Day 4

"It's Too Late."

We are so time conscious. We allow time to limit us and define for us what we're capable of or what God can do in our lives.

Today we're fasting from the thought that says, **"It's too late."**

It's often ingrained in us that it's too late to change, too late to start a new career, too late to save your marriage, too late to recover from a terrible mistake, too late to start over again, or too late to have a second chance.

The truth is: It's never too late!

When you realize that it's not too late, you have hope. You take action. You move forward.

LET'S CHANGE IT TODAY

1. **UN-DECIDE that it's too late for these things to change.** *Un-decide* that you can't recover. *Un-decide* that the damage is irreversible. It's NOT too late to turn your finances around, to recover from a tragedy or mistake, to surrender your life to God, to take better care of yourself; to change the way you see yourself, to apologize, or to break a bad habit.

2. **Meditate on the fact that God created time, and He can multiply it.** The earth and sun stood still in Joshua 10:12–13. "And Joshua said in the sight of Israel, 'Sun, stand still.' So the sun stood still, and the moon stopped." Joshua had control over time, for God's purpose. We need to start thinking that way—that we have control over our time, rather than it having control over us!

3. **Think about the great cloud of witnesses for whom it wasn't too late.**

    It wasn't too late for Abraham and Sarah to become parents at 99 and 90 years old.

    It wasn't too late for Peter after he denied the Lord three times.

    It wasn't too late for the woman caught in adultery (John 8:1–11), the woman with the issue of blood (Mark 5:25–34), or the man who was lame at the pool of Bethesda for 38 years (John 5:1–10).

4. **Embrace grace. Lamentations 3:22–33 says, "His mercy is new every morning . . ."** Hebrews 4:15 says, "Come boldly to the throne of grace to receive mercy and grace in your time of need." *Mercy* is when God doesn't give us the judgment that we do deserve, and *grace* is when God gives us the goodness that we don't deserve.

5. **Rid yourself of excuse-making.** God doesn't accept excuses, but He gives lots of grace! We might feel low self-esteem or have a disability as Moses did. He had a speech impediment, but God gave him chance after chance to be used to deliver God's people.

6. **Ask God for more time and another chance.** Hezekiah did this in 2 Kings 20:1–6. When Hezekiah asked for a second chance, God told him, "I have heard your prayer . . . Surely I will heal you . . . And I will add to your days fifteen years." If he did it for Hezekiah, He will do it for you!

THINK IT AND SAY IT

It is not too late for things to improve in my life and radically turn around. I believe in the God of second chances. I can recover, and there is nothing that God won't turn around in my life. God created time, and He can multiply it for me. I am not controlled by time. By God's grace, I control it, in Jesus' Name!

Day 5
"I Am Afraid."

Today we're fasting from the granddaddy of all wrong thinking: **"I'm afraid."**

Fear is at the root of just about every negative thing that happens in our lives. We're afraid of failing; afraid of being alone or rejected; afraid of running out of money; afraid that people will let us down; afraid that we won't find a spouse, or the one we found will leave us (or in some cases that they WON'T leave us—ha, ha).

All fear is rooted in the core belief that God's Word won't work. For example, the fear of not having enough is rooted in the fear that Philippians 4:19 isn't true. If you believe that "God will supply all your needs according to His riches, . . ." then fear leaves.

LET'S CHANGE IT TODAY

1. **Meditate on the fact that God's Word is true.** In John 17:17, Jesus said, "Thy Word is truth." What God says is fact—whether you feel it, see it, or you have ever experienced it.

2. **Consider God's track record.** 1 Kings 8:56 says, ". . . He has done all that He promised. Every word has come true of all His good promise . . ." (NLV).

Fear leaves when you can rely on something that can't fail. God has never failed to fulfill His promises. There are over 1000 predictions or prophecies in the Bible—promises that God made before they happened. The chances of merely 17 of these coming to pass is 1 out of 450 billion x 1 billion x 1 trillion! Yet, not one of these promises have failed.

3. **Accept the truth that what we fear comes upon us.** In Job 3:25, Job feared that his children would curse God, and that's what happened. When you realize fear has the power to produce negative results, you stop dabbling in it. When a child learns what fire can do, he no longer plays with matches!

4. **Perfect love casts out fear.** (1 John 4:18) Flood your mind with thoughts of love—God's love for you and what He was willing to do to rescue you. If He would die for you while you were in sin and separated from God, there's just nothing He wouldn't do for you! Think on that, and fear will leave.

5. **There is a promise from God's Word for every need you will ever experience.** In fact, there are over 7000 promises in the Bible. That's 7000 solutions to life's problems! For example, there is a promise of protection in Psalm 91:1–12, which delivers you from the fear of evil, sickness, or tragedy.

6. Pause and dwell on the fact that God is with you. Psalm 23:4 says, "Though I walk through the valley of the shadow of death, I will fear no evil—for YOU ARE WITH ME." God's presence is the secret to a fear-free life. All fear ultimately is a sense of God's absence or our separation from God. By contrast, a sense of God's presence delivers us from fear. Hebrews 10:19 says we enter the holy place of His presence by the blood of Jesus. You are in His presence now—therefore, fear not!

THINK IT AND SAY IT

God's Word is true, whether I feel it or not. He has kept all of His promises and has never failed.

I am in God's presence by the blood of Jesus; therefore, because He is with me, I will fear *no evil!*

God loves me perfectly, casting out all fear. I have power, love, and a sound mind, in Jesus' Name!

Day 6

"I Feel So Angry."

Today, we are fasting from anger—thoughts like, **"I feel so angry,"** or, **"They make me so mad."**

Anger is a powerful emotion that obviously can hurt ourselves and others. It leads to bad decisions, damaged relationships, stress, and physical sickness.

LET'S CHANGE IT TODAY

1. **Discover the power within you.** Remember, anger comes from a sense of powerlessness. When we feel powerless to change something, we get afraid, leading to anger. 2 Timothy 1:7 says God has not given us a spirit of fear, but power, love, and a sound mind. Meditate on this verse. You have power.

2. **Listen quickly and speak slowly.** James 1:19 says: be quick to hear, slow to speak, then the result is that you will be slow to anger! Follow this simple pattern, and anger will lose its grip.

3. **Realize that anger does not work.** It doesn't produce or achieve anything. James 1:20 says, "For the anger of man does not *achieve* (work, produce) the righteousness of God." If you had an employee that didn't work, produce, or achieve, you would fire

them, right? *Fire* your anger from your life. It doesn't achieve anything.

4. **Deal with unresolved conflict *today!*** Ephesians 4:26 says, "Do not let the sun go down on your anger." Make peace with whomever you have something against today. Don't let it fester. You'll be amazed at how much less you will feel angry.

5. **It's OK to feel anger, but direct it the right way—toward the devil.** Notice, the verse goes on to say, "Don't give the devil an opportunity to work." The devil wants you to blame others for your anger. But realize, there's no one to blame but the slithering devil! And like a machine gun soldier who just discovered the enemy, turn your weapons completely on him. Use your anger to resist the devil, speaking the Word with an aggressive force, and cut that old dragon to pieces!

6. **Get the whole picture.** So often, the reason we get mad or afraid is because we only see a snapshot of what's really going on. As soon as anger comes, ask God to open your eyes to see the big picture. He did it for Elisha's servant (2 Kings 6:16–17). He will do it for you!

THINK IT AND SAY IT

I am free from the power of anger. I have power over it! I have power, love and a sound mind. I will not act rashly, but choose to listen quickly and speak slowly.

I say to anger: *You are fired!*

I refuse to blame anyone for my angry feelings. I will use my aggressive feelings against the devil, speaking the Word of God and resisting him *firmly* in my faith today, in Jesus Name!

Day 7
"I'm Overwhelmed!"

Today we are fasting from the feelings and thoughts that say, **"I'm overwhelmed!"**

Everything you see in this world was created by God in six days. He's in the business of getting a lot accomplished in little time. And He lives in you! You don't have to carry your burden alone. Most people don't understand what Jesus meant when He said, "Take My yoke upon you" (Matthew 11:29).

A yoke is a harness placed upon two oxen. It causes them to plow together. So, when one gets weak or overwhelmed, he can continue by being pulled by the other. When we feel weighed down, we need to remember, we are yoked to Him. Jesus is attached to us and will carry the load for us.

LET'S CHANGE IT TODAY

1. **Cast your cares upon God. He will care for you.** (1 Peter 5:7) How? Be honest. Tell him what's wrong. Ask Him to carry it for you and believe He will. Remember, after you give Him your cares, don't run to pick them back up. Trust Jesus to carry the load for you.

2. **See yourself attached, or yoked, to God.** He holds you up and pulls you when you are weak and overwhelmed. You are one with Him. When you feel weak and burdened, remember that He is carrying you.

3. **Begin to believe that you can handle anything.** Start believing this today. Mark 9:23 says, "All things are possible for those who believe."

4. **Feast on this thought: Nothing is too difficult for God.** (Jeremiah 32:17) If nothing is too difficult for Him, and He lives in you, then nothing is too difficult for you. You will make it!

5. **God will complete those things that concern you** (Psalm 138:8) As you surrender those concerns to God, they become His responsibility. He will complete, fulfill, perfect, and bring those things to pass. He will lift your burden and finish what He started in your life.

THINK IT AND SAY IT

I can handle anything today, because I am yoked to Jesus. Today I refuse to be overwhelmed. I cast all my cares on Jesus. He cares for me and will carry my load.

Nothing is too difficult for God. Therefore, I declare that nothing is too difficult for me today! He is the author and finisher of my faith, in Jesus' Name!

Day 8

"God Is Mad at Me."

Today we are fasting from the thought that says, **"God is mad at me."**

Many people think the reason bad things are happening is because God is mad or against them. Or perhaps you don't think He's overtly against you, but that He's just not aggressively helping you. If you think God is mad at you, you'll feel discouraged and rejected. You won't expect good things to happen.

Let's take this thought captive. The word, *captive,* means: "to conquer with a sword." We conquer wrong thinking with the sword of God's Word!

LET'S CHANGE IT TODAY

1. **God is not mad at you; He is mad about you!** This is something I started saying many years ago when I discovered God's love. When you accept this thought, you will have confidence, expectation, and peace. How do I know this is true? Romans 8:38–39 says, "Nothing can separate you from the love of God . . . " You are forgiven (Ephesians 1:7), and you are LOVED (1 John 4:10).

2. **Think this new thought: God loves me as much as He loves Jesus.** In John 17:23, Jesus says to the

Father, ". . . that the world may know that You sent Me, and *loved them, as much as You have loved Me."* What an amazing truth. God loves you as much as He loves Jesus!

3. **He thinks precious thoughts about you *all the time!*** Psalm 139:17–18 says, "How precious are Your thoughts toward me, O God . . . If I should count them, they would outnumber the sand. When I awake, I am still with You!"

4. **What God said to Jesus is the same for you.** "You are My beloved Son. In You, I am well-pleased" (Mark 1:11). Hallelujah! He doesn't sound mad at Jesus. He sounds mad about Him! Well, 1 John 4:17 says, "As He is, so are we."

5. **There is nothing God is holding back from you.** Romans 8:32 says, "He who did not spare His own Son, but delivered Him up for us all, how shall He not also with Him freely give us all things." Rejoice in this truth!

6. **You are not condemned.** Romans 8:1 says, "There is no condemnation for those who are in Christ Jesus. . ." God approves of you because of your faith in Jesus, not because you have done everything right. God's love for you is non negotiable. Jeremiah 31:3 says He loves you with an everlasting love. It is unstoppable love!

THINK IT AND SAY IT

God is not mad at me; He is mad about me. He loves me as much as Jesus. He thinks precious thoughts about me all the time. I am His beloved, and He is mine!

There is nothing God is holding back from me. He didn't hold back His best, therefore He won't hold back the rest.

I refuse to be condemned. I am forgiven. I reject the thought that He is mad at me or against me. God is for me and not against me. His love toward me is unstoppable, in Jesus' Name!

Day 9

"I Don't Have Enough."

Most people know the benefits of fasting from food, but fasting from wrong thinking is unprecedented–until now! As you continue this amazing journey and tap into this power, you will be transformed!

Today we are fasting from the thought that says, **"I don't have enough."**

This is a mind-set that says, "I don't have enough money. I don't have enough time. I don't have enough friends. I don't have enough education . . ."

These thoughts build an invisible fence that keep you in the backyard of lack and deficiency.

LET'S CHANGE IT TODAY

1. **Believe in God's abundant provision.** Our God calls Himself: El Shaddai, the God of more than enough. We have more than enough of God living inside of us (Romans 8:11). Let's stop thinking in terms of *not enough* and start thinking in terms of *more than enough*.

2. **Think multiplication.** God said: Be fruitful and multiply. He is a multiplier, and so are you. Believe in the God of multiplication!

In 1 Kings 17, there was more than enough for Elijah and the widow.

In Exodus 16, there was more than enough for the children of Israel every day.

In John 6, there was more than enough bread left over after Jesus fed the 5000.

In Mark 5, there was more than enough anointing to heal Jairus, the woman with the issue of blood, and all the people that were sitting nearby!

3. **Think: apple orchard.** An apple seed becomes an apple orchard. One little seed becomes more than enough apples for a whole community! Believe in the power of a seed.

4. **Seed meets need.** Remember, even God cannot multiply a seed that you don't sow. Sow a seed (Mark 4:26).

5. **Be patient.** Farmers understand there is seed, time, and harvest (Genesis 8:22). Don't forget that *time* is the connector between the seed and the harvest.

6. **God is not trying to get something *from* you; He's trying to get something *to* you.** Trust. Let go. As you let go of what you have in your hand, you are able to receive what God is trying to put in your hand! Give, and it will be given back to you in good measure (Luke 6:38).

THINK IT AND SAY IT

I always have enough, because Philippians 4:19 says, God shall supply *all* my needs, according to His riches. I always have enough, because My God is more than enough. I believe that seeds meet needs. I am a sower, and therefore I am a reaper. God is a multiplier, and so am I.

I am called to be fruitful and multiply. God is multiplying every good seed that I have ever sown. As I give, He gives back to me good measure, pressed down, shaken together, and running over, in Jesus' Name!

(Pg. 67
Pg. 119)

Day 10

"God Is Far from Me."

Today we are fasting from the thought that says, **"God is far from me."**

We must learn to not only discern between right and wrong, but we must discern between *right* and *almost right*.

It's *almost right* to ask God to come down and help us. It sounds holy. It sounds humble. But you will truly be free when you discover, *He is already here. Emmanuel* means, "God WITH us." When Jesus came to the earth, He put an end to the separation between God and man.

Separation between us and God is a myth. It's an illusion. The devil wants us to believe it to keep us powerless. We *were* separated from God through our sin (Isaiah 59:2), but Jesus *took away* the sin through His blood. Therefore, the moment we are born again, there is *no separation* anymore. We sometimes feel that He is so far away, but He is not. He is here. He is there.

LET'S CHANGE IT TODAY

1. **Psalm 46:1 says, "He is an ever-present help in times of trouble."** Wow! You have to love this thought. Have you ever had times of trouble? But

notice, He is ever-present. Then, it says, *help* in times of trouble. It is His ever-presence that brings us help in times of trouble.

2. **Take Him at His Word.** Jesus said in Matthew 28:20, "Lo, I am with you always; even to the end of the age." There is no way to misinterpret this verse. Jesus is with YOU always. That has to warm your heart and comfort you.

3. **Christianity is not a life of attainment, but a life of recognition.** Philemon 6 says, "that your faith might become effective, through the *acknowledgment* of those things which are already in you, in Christ Jesus." Many people focus on attaining God's presence and God's blessing. But the Scripture is clear: Acknowledge. Recognize He is already in you. His gifts are already in you!

4. **Christianity is not us *finding* God.** It's that Jesus came and found us, spilled His blood to cleanse us from all unrighteousness, took us into His arms, and breathed His very Spirit into us. Now He lives in every person that has accepted Him as their Savior and Lord. Romans 8:11 tells us that the Spirit of God lives in us!

5. **Resist the temptation to pray, "God, come down and help me," or, "Send Your Spirit."** He has

already come. He has already sent His Spirit. Our battle is to believe this whether we feel His presence or not. He is in us!

6. **It's not us living *for* God. It's us living from God.** Galatians 2:20 says, "It is no longer I who live, but Christ lives in me." David said in Psalm 139:7–9, "Where can I flee from Your presence? If I go to heaven, You are there. If I make my bed in Sheol, You are there. If I take the wings of the dawn and dwell in the uttermost parts of the sea, even *there* Your hand will lead me, and Your right hand will hold me."

THINK IT AND SAY IT

I am not separated from God in any way. He is an ever-present help in my time of trouble. His ever-presence brings me help! I recognize that He is already in me. That's what makes my faith work.

God is not far off. He is right here, right now. I am surrounded by His love and enveloped in His presence. Therefore I am not afraid. I am not trying to live FOR God; I am living FROM Him. His power is in me. His presence is in me. His love is in me. And nothing can ever separate me from the love of God, which is in Christ Jesus my Lord! Amen.

Day 11

"My Life Is out of Control!"

Today we are fasting from the thought that says, **"My life is out of control!"**

That's what the devil wants you to think. When you think this way, you get discouraged. You lose hope.

LET'S CHANGE IT TODAY

1. **Think above and look down!** Think from a higher point of view. Then: Look down at life rather than **up** at it. When Elisha's servant saw from **above,** he realized there were more for him than those against him (2 Kings 6:14–17). Notice, God didn't add any chariots. They were always there. Elisha's servant just couldn't see them until God opened his eyes. Ask Him to open yours today.

2. **You are BIGGER than the situation.** Greater is He that is in you—that makes you big! (1 John 4:4) Remember, how YOU see yourself is how life will see you. That's how the enemy will see you. The 10 spies said, "We became like grasshoppers *in our own sight, and so we were in their sight.*" (Numbers 13:33) See yourself bigger than the mountain, and it will move when you tell it to!

3. **The best day of your life is the day you decide your choices are your own; therefore, your life is your own.** No more excuses. No one to blame. Remember the lame man who for 38 years sat at the pool of Bethesda? He stayed in his condition because he told Jesus what he had believed for all those years: "I have no one to help me" (John 5:7). *Decide to own your choices,* and you will own the life God wants you to have.

4. **Focus on the inside, not the outside.** Jesus had peace on the *inside* asleep in the boat. That's why He could speak to the storm on the outside: *peace be still* (Mark 4:37–39). If you're like me, there are several things on the outside that are not fully under control. But your job is to get control of the inside. That's what this Fast from Wrong Thinking" is about. You are in control, *if* you control your thought life.

5. **Take control of your day, one thought at a time.** Don't feel overwhelmed. You don't have to have it all together today! Isaiah 28:13 says that we build God's Word and God's thoughts in our lives, "line upon line, precept upon precept."

THINK IT AND SAY IT

I am in control of my life, because I am in control of my thoughts. I rule my life by ruling my thoughts. My thoughts liberate my emotions, my health, my relationships, and my whole life.

I have control of the choices I make.

I will not stay in a defeated, lonely, sick, depressed condition another day of my life. I know the thoughts of victory that I am developing on the inside will take care of my outside. This Fast from Wrong Thinking is working in me, in Jesus' Name!

Day 12
"I Can't Seem to Stop This Anxiety."

Today we're fasting from the thought that says, **"I can't seem to stop this anxiety."**

Some of the symptoms of anxiety include: heart palpitations, tension, fatigue, nausea, chest pain, shortness of breath, stomach aches, and headaches. You don't have to live this way.

LET'S CHANGE IT TODAY

1. **Treat anxiety as a signal rather as a condition.** It is a signal to pray, and prayer will change the thing you are facing (Philippians 4:6–7).

2. **More praying about *it* = less worrying about *it*.** James 5:16 says the prayer of the righteous avails much. Stop trying to SUBTRACT the anxiety. Instead, just ADD prayer the moment you feel it, and anxiety will leave!

3. **When panic attacks, attack back!** How do you attack anxiety and panic? By speaking God's Word out of your mouth (Proverbs 18:21).

4. **It's not your fault! Embrace this truth.** Don't blame yourself for feeling anxious. It's the thief that comes to steal, kill, and destroy. Stop beating yourself up, when you feel anxiety. Instead, beat up on the enemy, by speaking God's Word.

5. **Remember your value.** Because you are so valuable in God's eyes, He will care for you. (Matthew 6:26–31) Yes, He values you, because He paid for you with the blood of Jesus!

6. **Breathe praise to God** "Let everything that has breath, praise the Lord" (Psalm 150:6). Experts agree that breathing literally helps manage anxiety. But when you BREATHE praise to God, you don't just manage anxiety, you MASTER it (Philippians 4:6–7).

THINK IT AND SAY IT

Anxiety has lost its power over me. When I feel anxious, it is a signal to pray and praise God. When I add prayer, anxiety is subtracted. Because I am so valuable to God, I know that He will take care of me.

I attack panic by speaking the Word of God. The Prince of Peace lives inside of me, Therefore, I have peace guarding my heart and mind. I breathe praise to God today, in Jesus' Name!

Day 13

"I Just Can't See Things Getting Better."

Today we're fasting from the thought that says, **"I just can't see things getting better."**

No matter how bad it looks in your life or in the world, God has promised that YOUR life will get better!

LET'S CHANGE IT TODAY

1. ***Better* is God's idea.** As New Testament believers, we have a BETTER covenant (Hebrews 8:6). BETTER promises (Hebrews 8:6). BETTER things (Hebrews 12:24)—established by BETTER blood—the blood of Jesus. This is God's pattern.

2. **Expect your ending to be better than your beginning.** In Ezekiel 36:11, God says, ". . . I will do better for you than at your beginnings." HE WILL DO IT!

3. ***Better* is in your spiritual DNA.** You are designed by God to go from one degree of glory to another. *Better* is in you, as a child of God. 2 Corinthians 3:18 says, ". . . our lives become brighter and more beautiful . . . as God enters . . ." (The Message)

4. **You are the righteousness of God, in Christ** (2 Corinthians 5:21). And the path of the righteous gets brighter and brighter until the full day (when Jesus returns)! (Proverbs 4:18) Expect things to get better until Jesus comes . . . starting today.

5. **See yourself as God's beloved son or daughter.** "Bring the best robe and put it on *my son*." (Luke 15:22) See what God does for His sons and daughters? Love ALWAYS makes things better.

THINK IT & SAY IT

It is God's desire to make my life better and better! It is His idea. He will do better for me than at my beginning!

Getting better is in my DNA. I'm designed by God to get better spiritually, physically, emotionally, financially, and in my relationships. Everything is getting better and better in my life, beginning today! My path is getting brighter and brighter, until Jesus comes back! Amen.

Day 14

"It's Impossible."

Today we are fasting from the thought that says, **"It's impossible."**

Jesus said, "All things are possible to him who believes" (Mark 9:23).

What is in your life today that you have given up on or considered impossible? Whatever it is (provided it's legal!), don't ever give up. *Never, never, never* give up.

One Easter weekend, a major political story broke in America. The *New York Times* asked me, "Since this story is so big, will you be speaking about it at church on Easter?" "It certainly is a big story," I responded, "But SOMEONE RISING FROM THE DEAD IS EVEN BIGGER!" They then asked what I would specifically say about it. I answered, "If a man can rise from the dead, anything is possible!"

So today, let's fast from the thought that says, **"It's impossible."**

LET'S CHANGE IT TODAY

1. **Think about the resurrection every day.** This reveals the miraculous power of God to do anything!

We tend to save these thoughts for Easter, but we need to think about the resurrection *all the time*. It awakens hope and faith in the possibilities of God.

2. **Stop thinking or saying, "I can't believe that."** Cynicism and skepticism have filled our culture. We need to get out of the habit of questioning and doubting the possibility of things. When you think there is no way, remember that JESUS IS THE WAY!

3. **Deal with the real problem.** It's not whether God will help. It's whether we believe. The man with the demon-possessed son came to Jesus and said, "If you can do anything, help us . . ." Jesus responded and said, "If you can believe . . ." See? It's not whether God can do it. It's whether we can believe it. And remember that faith comes from hearing God's Word (Romans 10:17).

4. **You are bigger than a mountain.** Believe that your words move mountains. Matthew 17:20 says, "You shall say to this mountain, 'Remove from here to there,' and it shall remove; and nothing shall be impossible to you." That's big!

5. **Meditate on people who had an impossible turnaround.** Abraham was 99 years old when he had a son. Sarah was 90! Moses parted the Red Sea. The

list goes on and on. Find those people in the Bible and fill your mind with their testimonies. Hebrews 12:1 says, "We have a great cloud of witnesses surrounding us . . ." If it could happen for them, it can happen for you, and *it will*.

6. **God CAN'T lie.** There is only ONE THING in this world that is impossible: it's impossible for God to lie (Hebrews 6:18). Don't throw away your confidence in God's promises. He will fulfill them.

THINK IT AND SAY IT

All things are possible for me, because I believe God's Word. All of His promises are possible because all His promises are "Yes"; and He can't lie.

Jesus is the WAY when it seems like there is no way. Faith comes as I hear God's Word; and faith moves the impossible mountain as I speak God's Word today, in Jesus' Name!

Day 15
"I Feel Guilty."

Today we're fasting from the thought that says, **"I feel guilty."**

We've all had thoughts that try to make us feel guilty, such as: "You don't do enough. You're not good enough. You don't say the right things. You don't take care of yourself. You don't measure up. You don't do as much for others as you should. You eat too much."

This line of thinking produces guilt, which leads to self-hatred, anger toward others, bad decisions, harsh words, procrastination and fear.

LET'S CHANGE IT TODAY

1. **Jesus declares you *not guilty*.** This doesn't mean that you've never sinned or done wrong. This means that He washed away all your sin and guilt with His blood. The Word of God declares Jesus as our guilt offering, thus declaring us free from guilt (Hebrews 7:27).

2. **See what God sees.** Accept Colossians 1:22, which says that through Jesus' blood, "He presents you holy and faultless and unblamable in the Father's eyes." When God sees you, He sees Jesus—like when Jacob

went before his father Isaac with the hair, skin, and scent of his brother. The father saw Jacob as if he were Esau. And He sees you as if you were Jesus—without guilt.

3. **Meditate on Job 10:7.** "According to your knowledge, *I am indeed not guilty . . .*" (NASB) When a person is born again, they are cleansed of sin and guilt by the blood of Jesus, and therefore *not guilty.*

4. **When you blow it, don't deny it.** Admit it. Confess it. 1 John 1:9 says, "If you confess your sin, He is faithful and just to forgive you and to *cleanse you from all unrighteousness.*"

5. **It's already done!** Believe that it is already done. The last words of Jesus on the cross were, "It is finished." At that moment, the price was paid for your sin and guilt. Hebrews 1:3 says, "He cleansed us from our sin."

6. **Stop thinking that you have to feel guilty to be forgiven.** Sometimes we think we owe it to people to feel guilty and bad for everything. Stop thinking that. You don't owe anyone. Don't think guilt somehow pays for something. The blood of Jesus paid it all. When we feel like we owe God guilt or we owe it to others to wallow in guilt, it's an insult to His blood.

7. Stop beating yourself up about what you haven't done. We often punish ourselves with self-condemnation. We will *never* do enough for God. That's why Jesus did it all. *He paid* for sin, the curse, and our failure. *Our job is to believe.*

THINK IT AND SAY IT

Jesus has declared me *not guilty*. Even when I feel I don't do enough, or that I'm not good enough, God says that *faith in Him is enough*.

I don't have to feel guilty to be forgiven. I am forgiven by faith in Jesus.

Today I stop beating myself up about all that I've done, or haven't done.

I don't have to be perfect. He already is; therefore, I rest my faith in Him, in Jesus' Name!

Day 16

"It's Just So Hard to Be a Christian."

Today we are fasting from the thought that says, **"It's just so hard to be a Christian."**

We are going to break this mentality once and for all, because it is the single most often misunderstood concept that is keeping believers defeated.

Jesus said to take His yoke because it's easy and His burden is light (Matthew 11:30). That's the grace of God! He did the heavy lifting, and now our job is to enter into His rest.

LET'S CHANGE IT TODAY

1. **It's not hard to be something you already are.** Jesus made you a Christian, and there's nothing that can change that. You're a new creation! (2 Corinthians 5:17) You are already more than a conqueror! You don't have to TRY to be a human. You are one! In the same way: You ARE a Christian!

2. **It is He who made us, and not we ourselves.** (Psalm 100:3) *Selah*—pause and think on that. HE MADE YOU A CHRISTIAN. And you can't undo what God has done.

3. **Jesus did it all.** When He said, "It is finished," in John 19:30, He meant: "The debt is paid; the sentence is served; the victory is won! I did everything necessary for you to be saved and at peace." Now, just believe it.

4. **Start realizing "Christ-ian" means "Christ-IN".** He is in you. It's *impossible* for you to fail at being a Christian, when the anointing, the Christ is at work within you (2 Corinthians 13:5, Colossians 1:27, Galatians 2:20).

5. **His yoke is easy.** Reverse your thinking. Think, "It's easy to be a Christian." His yoke is *easy*. His burden is *light*. (Matthew 11:30) You are yoked/connected/hitched to Him!

6. **Rest in the fact that you don't have to be perfect.** God is not holding you to a perfect standard. Jesus is your perfection. Just *rest* in this truth!

THINK IT AND SAY IT

It is easy to live the Christian life, because God already made me more than a conqueror. Jesus did it all!

His life is in me. His love is in me. His power is in me. His Spirit is in me. Therefore, I cannot fail as a Christian! I am not alone, and never will be.

I am yoked to Him, and that's why I can enjoy my relationship *with* God, rather than strive to fulfill a duty *for* God. I am free, in Jesus' Name!

(Pg. 68)

Day 17

"The Future Is Fearful and Uncertain."

With random acts of violence, economic problems, instability around the world, the future for you, or your children, can seem anything but bright. But that's all about to change!

Today we are fasting from the thought that says, **"The future is fearful and uncertain."**

LET'S CHANGE IT TODAY

1. **Realize your future is a *gift* from God.** Jeremiah 29:11 says, ". . . I know the plans I have for you . . . to GIVE you a future . . ." You see, God *gives* you a future, and everything He gives is *good and perfect*. Your good and perfect future is on its way. Receive it!

2. **You can KNOW what the future holds.** The Holy Spirit will show you. John 16:13 says the Holy Spirit will reveal to you the things to come. Ask Him to show you what is to come and trust Him to prepare you for it.

3. **Your future is in your seeds.** Our future is not determined by random luck, but rather by the

seeds we sow. God gave us seedtime and harvest to eliminate fear and to shape our future. (Genesis 8:22) Plant good seeds today for your tomorrow.

4. **Receive the wisdom of God.** All you have to do is ask (James 1:5). Proverbs 22:3 says that a wise man FORESEES what is coming and takes action. Wisdom empowers us to foresee. We act, rather than react. Ask God for wisdom today.

5. **Take Inventory of what you have in stock.** 2 Timothy 1:7 says God hasn't given the spirit of fear, but He has given power, love, and a sound mind. You are loaded with the tools to be free from fear.

6. **God's love for you is perfect.** One reason His love is perfect is because it is always accompanied with a gift. "God so loved the world that He GAVE . . ." There will never be any lack when you believe God's love for you. 1 John 4:18 says, "There is no fear where love exists. Rather, perfect love banishes all fear . . ." (ISV)

THINK IT AND SAY IT

I receive my GREAT future as a gift from God! I expect a fear-free life and a fear-free future. I invite the Holy Spirit to disclose to me the things to come, so I will not be caught off guard.

My seeds determine my future; therefore, I know what kind of harvest is coming. I have not been given the spirit of fear; but I have power, love, and a sound mind to shape my future.

God's love for me is perfect. It lacks nothing. Therefore I lack nothing; and all fear must leave my life now, in Jesus' Name!

Day 18

"Something Bad Is Going to Happen to Me or My Family."

The fallen world we live in is full of tragedy and suffering. News concerning violence, terror, and unexplainable disasters occurs much too often. When things like this happen, it is easy for fear to creep in and make us think we are sitting ducks for Satan or twisted people to strike at any time.

But *do not open the door* to the expectation of evil!

Today we are fasting from the thought that says, **"Something bad is going to happen to me or my family."**

Of course, we must have compassion for those who have suffered; but we cannot allow what has happened to others to create our expectations, and consequently, cause us to live a life full of fear.

LET'S CHANGE IT TODAY

1. **Believe God's promise:** Psalm 91:10, in the Message translation, really brings this Scripture to light: "Evil can't get close to you; harm can't get through the door." Then, in verse 11, it goes on to say, "He ordered His angels to guard you wherever you go." Believe it.

2. **Embrace this thought: "No weapon formed against me shall prosper."** Isaiah 54:17 clearly tells us that weapons will be formed against us, but *they shall not prosper*. We will always have adversity, because we have an enemy. But the enemy's weapons are powerless as we trust the promise of God's divine protection.

3. **Begin to speak the Word.** There is nothing stronger to combat the spirit of fear than you speaking the Word of God out of your mouth. Fill your heart with God's promises of provision and protection and declare them out loud.

4. **Know that God brings His Word to pass.** Jeremiah 1:12 says, "I am watching over My Word to perform it." Everything God has spoken concerning you is being carefully attended to by God Himself. He will keep His promises and bring His Word to pass.

5. **Expect something good to happen to you and your family.** Embrace the promise of Psalm 23 that His goodness will follow you *all* the days of your life. Start today. It takes as much energy to believe bad things are going to happen as it does to believe good things are coming your way. Expect the good!

THINK IT AND SAY IT

I believe the promises of God. Evil cannot come close to me. God guards me everywhere I go. I fill my heart and mouth with the good things God says about me.

He is watching over His Word to perform it in my life; therefore, I expect something good to happen.

I choose to expect only good. His goodness is following me today and every day, in Jesus' Name!

(Pg. 153)

Day 19

"How Could Something So Bad Ever Turn Into Something Good?"

Today we fasting from the thought that says, **"How could something so bad ever turn into something good?"**

We've all thought that at one time or another.

LET'S CHANGE IT TODAY

1. **God is in the business of turning bad into good.** (Romans 8:28) He doesn't *cause everything*, but He can cause everything to turn into something good. He turns the curse into a blessing, because He loves you! (Deuteronomy 23:5)

2. **That's the favor of God.** A turnaround is an act of God's favor. He turns things to your advantage, because of His grace—not because we deserved it. Psalms 5:12 says, favor surrounds the righteous (in Christ), like a shield. Expect your turnaround today!

3. **Think: resurrection!** If Jesus rose from the dead, your bad situation can turn around, too. Listen to this: "We felt like . . . it was all over for us. As it

turned out, it was the best thing that could have happened. Instead of trusting in our own strength to get out of it, we were forced to trust God totally—not a bad idea, since He's the God who raises the dead!" (2 Corinthians 1:9 MSG)

4. **Expect this *bad* thing to become the *best* thing that ever happened.** (Look at verse above.)

5. **Accept the fact that you don't *deserve* this supernatural favor.** That's what makes it *favor:* we don't deserve it. (Ephesians 2:8) But God keeps giving it freely. Expect!

6. **See God as your turnaround specialist.** There are experts in business who come into a company and transform the company, saving it from disaster and loss. THAT'S THE GOD WHO LIVES IN YOU. He's YOUR turnaround specialist. He turns sadness into joy (Psalm 30:11); darkness to light; the curse into a blessing . . .

THINK IT AND SAY IT

I expect my turnaround, beginning today. No matter how bad my situation is, God is my turnaround specialist! He's in the business of turning things into something good.

This kind of favor surrounds me like a shield—not because I deserve it, but because of what Jesus did for me. That's the favor of God! He's the God who raises the dead, so He can turn this around. I trust Him today, in Jesus' Name!

Day 20
"It's Too Hard to Find God's Will."

Today we're fasting from the thought that says, **"The will of God is such a mystery."** Or, **"It's too hard to find God's will."**

Many people struggle to find the will of God, only to be frustrated and confused. Can we ever be sure of the will of God? We can. And I believe this will help.

LET'S CHANGE IT TODAY

1. **Change the way you look at the Bible.** It's not a book of rules. Let's look at the Bible as a love letter, a description of who we are in Christ, and a collection of divine seeds for the harvests of life.

2. **Today you must see the Bible *as a will*.** It is God's last will and testament (Hebrews 9:15–17). Enclosed in the Bible is everything Jesus, after dying, has left to His loved ones—that's you and me!

3. **Remember, a will goes into effect when someone dies.** Hebrews 9:17 says, "because a will is in force only when somebody has died; it never takes effect while the one who made it is living." Because Jesus died, He has left us with all of His possessions.

4. **See yourself in God's will *now*.** Through Jesus' blood and His death, God has placed us in His will.

5. **The Gospel includes forgiveness AND an inheritance that now belongs to us** (Acts 26:18). Read the Scriptures to discover your inheritance and know what belongs to you now, in Christ.

6. **Now, take the pressure off yourself in trying to discover what to do, and focus on discovering what is yours in Christ.** This will change how you look at yourself and how you live.

7. **Don't try to find the will of God.** It will find you! Just meditate on God's Word. As you renew your mind to His thoughts and promises, you end up in the will of God (Romans 12:2).

THINK IT AND SAY IT

God has placed me in His will. I don't have to strive to find it. God's will is His covenant toward me, and His promised inheritance is mine through the blood of Jesus.

I will see the Bible as God's will toward me. I will read it to discover what belongs to me and who I truly am in Him, and the will of God will track me down, in Jesus' Name!

Day 21
"I Just Can't Forgive Myself."

Today we are fasting from the thought that says, **"I just can't forgive myself."**

The devil would love to keep us in condemnation for the things we have done or failed to do. He knows it paralyzes us and prevents us from making the impact that God created us for.

I once read of a young teenager who accidentally struck his little sister with a car, killing her in their driveway. As horribly tragic as that is, imagine the life-long challenge of this young man trying to forgive himself. Though few of us have faced something as tragic as this, we all need to overcome the thoughts that try to accuse us for what we have done.

LET'S CHANGE IT TODAY

1. **Realize that we only deserve forgiveness because of the blood of Jesus.** It's not because our mistakes never happened, or they weren't that bad. Receive God's mercy.

2. **It was that bad, but God is even more good!** James 2:13 says mercy triumphs over judgment. His mercy toward you trumps your judgment over yourself. In

Luke 22:34, Peter denied the Lord three times, and Jesus forgave him. Later, Peter preached the first sermon after Jesus rose from the dead, and 3000 people were saved in a day. Peter was able to forgive himself when he knew Jesus had accepted him. You have been accepted by God, no matter what you have done—simply by believing in His finished work on the cross.

3. **Give up your right to hold anything against yourself.** If God can forgive you, you can forgive yourself. His standard is absolute perfection, and He forgives you. Psalm 103:12 says, "As far as east is from west, so far has He removed our transgressions from us." As soon as you accept this truth, it becomes so much easier to forgive others.

4. **Stop rehearsing what you did.** It's done. It's over. Now accept the second chance (or third, or fourth) that God offers. Philippians 3:10 says, "forgetting what lies behind, and reaching forward..." Reaching forward starts in your thought life.

5. **Believe that guilt doesn't come from God.** He doesn't impose guilt on you to try to get you to stop doing something. Romans 2:4 says that it is His love and kindness that leads us to repentance. Guilt and shame come from the devil. Resist him firm in your faith. He will flee (1 Peter 5:9).

6. Give up *self-punishment*. Many people think subconsciously, "If I feel bad enough, I can pay for what I've done." Why should we pay the price that has *already* been paid? Stop beating yourself up. You're already forgiven. By trying to "pay for what we have done," we are doubting and insulting the very blood of Jesus, which has paid the price in full. Accept His free gift (Ephesians 1:7).

THINK IT AND SAY IT

I receive mercy today, because of the blood of Jesus. Though I didn't deserve it, God proclaims over me, that I am *not guilty!*

I give up my right today to hold *anything* against myself. I deserve to be punished, but Jesus took that punishment for me.

I reject the guilt and condemnation that the devil is trying to put on me. God is the God of second chances. The price for what I did or failed at has been paid in full by Jesus' blood! Amen.

Day 22

"I'm Inferior."

Today we are fasting from the thought that says, **"I'm inferior."**

Ever felt like that? Or inferiority's offspring: "I don't measure up"; "I feel small"; "I feel insignificant." It's time to get rid of this thinking.

LET'S CHANGE IT TODAY

1. **Take a look at the new seating chart.** (Ephesians 2:6) You don't have to *measure* up, because God has *raised* you up and seated you with Him in heavenly places!

2. **Stop disapproving of yourself.** You are approved by God *today* (Mark 1:11). You are accepted in the beloved (Ephesians 1:6). Believe it. When you believe God approves of you, you stop seeking it from others. And you stop beating yourself up!

3. **See yourself above only and not beneath.** (Deuteronomy 28:13) You are the head and not the tail. Remember, what you *see* is what will *be*.

4. **See yourself *big* today.** Replace the grasshopper image with the image of a giant! 1 John 4:4 says,

"Greater is He that is in you . . ." God is bigger than any mountain or problem, and He lives in you. For Him to fit inside of you makes you pretty huge (in the Spirit)!

5. **You have what it takes.** You have the mind of Christ (1 Corinthians 2:16), and you have a treasure in you (2 Corinthians 4:6). The devil wants you to think that others have what it takes to win, but you don't. That's a lie. Reject this lie with the truth of who you are.

6. **Imprint this on your heart and mind: Royalty destroys inferiority!** Acquaint yourself with your new bloodline. You are royalty in Christ. This makes you reign over life (Romans 5:17). When you know that you are made righteous and made royal by His blood, it makes you as confident and bold as a lion! (Proverbs 28:1) Believe it!

THINK IT AND SAY IT

I am seated with Jesus Christ in heavenly places. I am above only and not beneath. I am approved by God. I have what it takes. God has put a treasure in me and equipped me with the Holy Spirit and power to be up to any task.

I am not inferior to anyone or anything. I have the royal blood of Jesus running through my veins! I am His righteousness; and therefore, I am as bold and confident as a lion, reigning in this life, in Jesus' Name!

Day 23

"Happiness Is So Hard to Find."

Today we're fasting from the thought that says, **"Happiness is so hard to find."**

People have been looking for happiness—trying to buy it, trade for it, or discover it—since time began. But it's not hard to find.

LET'S CHANGE IT TODAY

1. **You don't have to find happiness.** It will find you! Jesus tells us in Matthew 6:33 that as we seek His kingdom ". . . all these things will be added to you." Expect happiness to be added to you as you put His kingdom first. How do you do that? Start each day planting the seed of God's Word in your life (Mark 4:26).

2. **Happy is the man who does not condemn himself.** (Romans 14:22) Refuse to tolerate condemnation another second of your life. Romans 8:1 says, *there is no condemnation.* Believe that Jesus freed you from condemnation; and happiness will come!

3. **Treat unhappiness as a signal to trust God.** Jeremiah 17:7 says happy is the man that trusts in the Lord. Declare that you trust Him today!

4. **The supreme happiness in life is the ASSURANCE that you are loved.** You can be sure God loves you—no matter what. Nothing can separate you from His love (Romans 8:38–39). Think on that.

5. **God will help you be happy today.** Psalm 146:5 says, "Happy is he whose help and hope are in the Lord." Ask for His help today. Ask Him for hope today. Believe you have received it, and joy will come.

6. **In His presence is *fullness* of joy.** (Psalm 16:11) Be mindful that you are in His presence *now*, by the blood of Jesus. (Hebrews 10:19) And the Holy Spirit lives in you! (Romans 8:11) It will change your view of life.

THINK IT AND SAY IT

I have the fullness of joy and happiness in life, because I am in God's presence, and the Holy Spirit lives in me. I walk in the supreme happiness of life, knowing that I am loved by God.

I refuse to condemn myself, because there is no condemnation in Christ Jesus. God will always help me, and my hope is in Him. Therefore, I am happy, in Jesus' Name!

Day 24

"It's Hopeless."

Your thought life is the gateway to your destiny!

God's purpose and will for your life doesn't start with a great dream or great effort on your part. It simply starts with right thinking. It begins with mind-sets that line up with God's way of thinking.

Today, we are FASTING from the thought that says, **"It's hopeless."**

When problems mount; society seems to be getting worse; or you continue to struggle in your home, finances, or health; it's easy to feel hopeless.

LET'S CHANGE IT TODAY

1. **See Hope as a *gift*.** Jeremiah 29:11 says that God *gives* you hope. It's a gift. It is not earned or deserved. When hope seems lost, just ask for this precious gift.

2. **God has a plan.** No matter how it looks, He has a master plan that includes getting you through whatever you're facing! Jeremiah 29:11 says, "I know what I'm doing. I have it all planned out . . ." (Message Bible). Trust God to carry out His plan in your life today.

3. **Your great future is a gift, too.** Accept a great future, as a gift, no matter what the present looks like now. God said His plan is ". . . to GIVE you a future and a hope" (Jeremiah 29:11b). He uses the word GIVE because your future is a gift. Ask Him to give you great future right now.

4. **Believe in the power of the Holy Spirit today.** Romans 15:13 says, "The God of Hope fills you with all joy and peace, through believing—that you may overflow with hope by the POWER of the Holy Spirit." Expect His power. And hope will come!

5. **Get some substance.** "Faith is the substance of things hoped for . . ." (Hebrews 11:1) Stand on *one* promise from God's Word today. That's what gives you substance—causing your hope to be substantial.

THINK IT AND SAY IT

My God is the God of hope. He never runs out; therefore, I never run out. Hope is a gift, and I ask for it and receive it right now. I trust God's plan will overtake my situation.

My future is great because God has it all planned out. I can't earn a great future because of all that I do; but I can receive a great future through God's great grace toward me!

The power of the Holy Spirit is working in me today, to flood me with overflowing hope, in Jesus' Name!

Day 25
"I'm Offended."

Today we are fasting from the thought that says, **"I'm offended."**

We all know what's it like to be treated wrongly or unfairly; to be talked about or lied about. It's easy to become offended and feel that we have the right to feel that way. But this is a destructive trap.

LET'S CHANGE IT TODAY

1. **Being offended traps *you*.** *Skandalon* (offense) is the trigger of a well-baited trap. When an animal touches the trigger of a snare, it is caught. When you are offended, you are the one caught in the trap. By thinking and knowing this, it will empower you to stay out of the traps.

2. **Being offended comes from self-righteousness.** We think, "How could they do that to me? I would never have done that!" But we have all sinned. (Romans 3:23) Embrace humility with the sure knowledge that you have failed, too. And *offense* loses its grip on you.

3. **You can't afford to *pay attention!*** 1 Corinthians 13:5 (Amplified Bible) says, "Love (God's love in us) is not touchy or fretful or resentful." Why? "Because

it **pays no attention** to a suffered wrong." We get offended when we pay attention to the wrong we have suffered. Stop paying attention.

4. **Take back control.** We let others control us when we pay *attention* to what they did to us.

5. **Express UP, not OUT.** Fully express your anger and hurt out loud to God. Tell Him how much it hurt. Forgive the offender (out loud to God) whether you feel anything or not; and ask Him to heal you.

6. **NOTHING CAN OFFEND YOU!** How is that possible? Psalm 119:165 says that those who love the Word have great peace, and nothing offends them. One of the meanings of the Greek word for "love" is "attachment." Attach yourself to what God says, and you'll detach from the power of what others have done or said to you. That's what it means to love God's Word.

THINK IT AND SAY IT

I am free from being offended. I am free from the emotions of offense, bitterness, and the right to feel mad. I will not be trapped by those feelings. I love God's Word. I attach myself to what He said and did.

I refuse to pay attention to the wrong done to me. I forgive and release those that have hurt me. I express my feelings to God, and I am healed, in Jesus' Name!

Day 26
"I Can't Stop."

Today we're fasting from the thought that says, **"I can't stop."**

Quitting a habit or sin can be one of the hardest things in life; but it becomes easy when we realize Jesus not only died to forgive our sins; but also to give us power over sin and to free us from being in bondage to anything.

LET'S CHANGE IT TODAY

1. **Stop trying to stop.** Instead, just continue to fast from wrong thinking. Proverbs 23:7 says, "As a man thinks, so is he." Your thoughts will shape your decisions; your decisions will shape your actions; your actions will shape your habits.

2. **Awaken to the grace of God.** Romans 6:14 tells us that sin does not have dominion over us . . . for we are not under the law, but under grace. Embrace the grace.

3. **Grace empowers.** Titus 2:11 says, "It is the grace of God that enables and instructs us to resist and deny ungodliness." Go to God's throne of grace right now and ask for His help (Hebrews 4:16).

4. **His yoke is easy.** You are yoked to Jesus (Matthew 11:28). That means He will carry the weight of your struggle and walk you through it.

5. **Change happens *to* you; not *by* you.** Romans 12:2 says, *Be* transformed. It is something that happens to you, as you renew your mind to God's Word. It's happening to you right now as you fast from wrong thinking!

6. **"There ain't no can't."** (Quote from Mickey to Rocky in the movie, *Rocky II*.) Get rid of "can't" from your vocabulary and your mind-set. You *can* do all things through Christ (Philippians 4:13).

THINK IT AND SAY IT

I am not under the bondage or control of any sin, habit, or problem in my life anymore. I am under the grace of God, giving me dominion over sin and temptation.

I am yoked to Jesus. Therefore, it is His strength that I walk in. As I renew my mind to the Word of God, I am being changed and transformed, in Jesus' Name!

Day 27

"I Haven't Done Enough to Get God to Answer My Prayers or Bless Me."

Today we're fasting from the thought that says, **"I haven't done enough to get God to answer my prayers or bless me."**

When things don't go our way, we sometimes have this nagging thought that we're not holy enough or haven't prayed enough to qualify us for God's blessing or favor.

LET'S CHANGE IT TODAY

1. **We get what Jesus deserves.** Romans 8:17 tells us that we are joint heirs with Jesus Christ. His inheritance is ours. 1 John 4:17 says, "As He is, so are we in this world." We deserved the curse, but instead we receive the blessing (Galatians 3:13).

2. **Be covenant-minded.** You have a covenant with God (Hebrews 8:12–13). A covenant is a contract—in this case, a contract that is guaranteed by the shed blood of Jesus Christ.

3. **Be grace-minded.** Grace is when God gives us what we don't deserve. Hebrews 4:15 says, "Therefore, let us draw near with confidence [boldly] to the throne of grace, so that we may receive mercy and find grace to help in time of need."

4. **Have confidence in God, not in yourself.** (1 John 3:20–21) Confidence and faith enable God to answer prayers in our lives.

5. **Reject condemnation.** It is our heart that condemns us for our mistakes and shortcomings. When we feel condemned, we lose confidence, and then we believe we can't receive anything from God. (Hebrews 10:35)

6. **Accept your freedom in Christ.** There is now NO condemnation for those who are in Christ! (Romans 8:1)

THINK IT AND SAY IT

I let go of the mind-set that tells me I'm not holy enough, or I haven't done enough to receive answered prayers. I receive His promises by faith. I am a joint heir with Jesus Christ.

I expect to get what He deserves, not what I deserve. The throne of His grace is always open! His river of lavish love-gifts are always flowing toward me! I receive His grace, freely and lavishly, in Jesus' Name!

Day 28
"I Don't Feel Loved."

We have embarked upon the most significant journey of our lives: fasting from wrong thinking. And today's thought is probably the most important one any of us ever deal with at a deep level.

Today, we are fasting from the thought that says, **"I don't feel loved."**

The number-one need in every human life is to be loved. Yet sadly, so few actually enjoy a life where they actually feel loved.

LET'S CHANGE IT TODAY

1. **God's not mad *at* you, He's mad *about* you!** Dispel the myth of an angry God. He poured out His wrath on Jesus while on the cross, so He could pour His love on you forever. "God is love" (1 John 4:8).

2. **Our feelings follow our thoughts.** Flood your mind with the thought, "My Heavenly Father tenderly loves me!" (John 16:27 AMP) You and God are inseparable. Nothing can separate you from Him or His love (Romans 8:37–39). Believe this with every fiber in your being!

3. **Recognize your value.** The value of a piece of art is not determined by the cost to make it, but rather by *how much someone would pay to have it.* God paid for us with the blood of Jesus. That makes us as valuable to God, as Jesus Himself! You are priceless!

4. **You don't have to earn something God has already given.** He loves you. That can't be earned. It is a gift from God. (John 3:16) Accept it. Your value is not determined by what you've done or not done. Just *be loved.*

5. **Reject the voices of rejection.** Look in the mirror and tell yourself that you are chosen by God, accepted, and outrageously loved! (Colossians 1:12, Ephesians 1:6)

6. **Know your calling.** By this, I'm not referring to your calling to serve in ministry or your profession. I'm talking about what God calls you. He calls you *His beloved* continually in the Bible. Do a word search. You are His beloved. So, *be loved!*

THINK IT AND SAY IT

God is not mad at me; He's mad about me! I am outrageously loved by Him!

His anger lasted for a moment on the cross, but His love and favor are for a lifetime!

My Heavenly Father tenderly loves me. Therefore, I will feel His love today! He continually calls me His beloved. Nothing can separate me from His love. I am valuable and priceless to Him. I am as valuable to God as Jesus is. I receive His love by faith, in Jesus' Name!

Day 29

"I Don't Think This Pain Will Ever Go Away."

Today we're fasting from the thought that says, **"I don't think this pain will ever go away."**

We all feel pain, whether physical or emotional: and though it feels at times like it may never go away, it can and will.

LET'S CHANGE IT TODAY

1. **Expect double for your trouble.** For every one mention of pain or sickness in the Bible, there are two mentions of health and healing. God has you covered!

2. **God designed you to get better.** If you're born again, you are the righteousness of God in Christ. And the righteous get better and better! (Proverbs 4:18) *You will get better.*

3. **The cross ends your pain.** Jesus bore *your* pain on the cross (Isaiah 53:4–5). 1 Peter 2:24 says, "He Himself bore our sins in His body on the cross, so that we might die to sin and live to righteousness; for by His wounds you were healed." Whenever you feel pain, take it to the cross and see Jesus taking it from you.

4. **Refuse to accept the pain or sickness.** Resist it; speak to it; and expect it to leave (1 Peter 5:7–8, Mark 11:23).

5. **Expect the Word of God to destroy the grip of pain and suffering in your life.** (Proverbs 4:20–22, Psalm 107:20) *There is no power that can prevail against the Word!*

6. **Expect God to grant your request!** Jabez was born in pain and named *Pain*. But he asked God to bless him and enlarge his territory; extend His hand and keep him from evil and pain. ". . . AND GOD GRANTED HIS REQUEST" (1 Chronicles 4:9–10). Jabez' pain was replaced with God's purpose. If He granted his request, He will grant yours!

THINK IT AND SAY IT

I refuse to tolerate pain in my life anymore. I am healed by the stripes of Jesus—spiritually, emotionally, and physically. I am getting better all the time.

I have the right to be healed by the blood of Jesus! The cross is the END to my pain. It is finished!

Lord, bless me indeed; and enlarge my territory. Let Your hand be with me, and keep me from evil and pain, in Jesus' Name!

Day 30

"My Life Is Not as Good as Others'."

So often, we battle thoughts of inferiority: "I'm not as blessed as others," "I'm not as attractive," "I'm not as successful," "My life is not as easy or fun." These types of thoughts lead to a major pity party and, eventually, to a spirit of depression. When we don't feel we measure up to others, we end up living below our own divine potential.

Today we're fasting from the thought that says, **"My life is not as good as others."**

LET'S CHANGE IT TODAY

1. **Step out of the comparison trap.** Society trains us to compare ourselves to one another, but 2 Corinthians 10:12 says that when we do this, we are without understanding. Understanding is what gives us the power to be happy and free (Proverbs 3:13–19). Stop looking at somebody else's money or figure, or their marriage or children. Thank God for what He has given you; and ask Him to fill the gaps in your life.

2. **Realize that God has reserved a special gift for you.** There is a portion for you no one can take (1 Samuel 9:23–24). There is a life and assignment reserved just

for you. The Bible says we all have different gifts—not competing gifts (Romans 12:6). We are as happy as we choose to be. Choose to be happy with the gifts and life God has given you.

3. **Live your life to please God.** 2 Corinthians 5:9 says, "We have as our ambition . . . to be pleasing to God." When you are busy living by faith, you no longer focus on what other people are experiencing or how you stack up against them. Stop living for the respect and esteem of others. Live by faith. That pleases God.

4. **Personalize God's promises.** Whenever you see one of God's promises in the Bible, just put your name in it. Believe that God is writing directly to you. Take, for example, Luke 12:32, which says, "Your Heavenly Father, has chosen gladly to give you the Kingdom." Personalize it: "*My* Heavenly Father has chosen gladly to give *me* the Kingdom!"

5. **Stop thinking backwards.** What I mean is: stop looking at what you *don't* have and start looking at what you DO have. You have eternal life. You are God's son or daughter. You have the rights of a child of God. When you think this way, you create an attitude of faith for all that God has for you.

THINK IT AND SAY IT

I am secure and confident in Christ. I have a special gift and treasure that God has placed within me. There is a portion and a place in God's Kingdom reserved for me. All of God's promises are personally for me.

I have a great life, because God is my Father, and He has chosen gladly to give me His Kingdom.

I thank God for what I DO have; and refuse to focus on what I don't have! I live by faith in God's promises; and therefore, I am pleasing to Him, in Jesus' Name!

Day 31
"I'm Stuck."

Today we are fasting from the thought that says, **"I'm stuck."**

We've all thought that at times, but it's a lie. There's always a way out of what you're in; or a way into what you've been kept out of.

The devil would love for you to believe you are stuck, and that there's no way out of the situation you're experiencing. He wants you discouraged, immobilized, and paralyzed.

LET'S CHANGE IT TODAY

1. **Believe in the ministry of the Holy Spirit in your everyday life.** Romans 8:26 says, "We don't always know how to pray as we should, but the Spirit intercedes for us . . ." No matter what your situation is, the Holy Spirit knows how to bring about God's will for your life, as you pray and thank Him.

2. **Think this thought today: PRAYER CHANGES THINGS.** There's nothing you can't impact through prayer. Prayer gets you unstuck. It gets you moving again. Prayer is powerful. "And all things, whatsoever you shall *ask* in prayer, believing, *you shall receive*" (Matthew 21:22).

3. **Believe that faith finds a way.** In Mark 2:1–5, the friends of the paralyzed man could not find a way into the house where Jesus was. They were stuck, *but they believed there was another way.* They went up on the roof and lowered him down through the ceiling tiles, and the man was healed. Why? Because faith found a way! If we don't think it, we won't look for it.

4. **Remember, Jesus is the fourth man in the fire.** When it seemed like the three men in Daniel 3 were going to be burned in the fiery furnace, Jesus showed up! What was an impossible situation was made possible, because Jesus was with them. And He is with you now!

5. **Jesus is your way.** "I am the way, the truth, and the life" (John 14:6). He is the way when there just seems to be no way. *He is your way* out of whatever situation you are in. Expect Him to make a way.

6. **Just think: Next step.** When Jesus was tempted to not go to the cross, the Bible says, "He went forward a little . . ." (Mark 14:35). When you feel stuck, like there's nothing you can do, just take a step. Don't think about all the steps. Just take the next one. In a relationship, the first step may be just saying you're sorry. If it's finances, maybe it's just cutting one area of spending or giving one extra offering. Move forward a little!

THINK IT AND SAY IT

The Holy Spirit is interceding for me when I feel stuck. He is moving in me and through me.

I think and believe there is always a way. Even when it seems like there is no way, Jesus is the Way.

He is with me no matter what fire I'm facing. When I feel stuck, I will think about one step I can take that will move me toward healing, blessing, and God's will for my life, in Jesus' Name!

Day 32
"This Problem Is Too Big!"

Today, we're fasting from the thought that says, **"This problem is too big."**

We all have problems, and they can seem overwhelming. They can seem too big for us to handle.

LET'S CHANGE IT TODAY

1. **The problem is not the problem.** When the disciples' boat was sinking, they thought the problem was the wind and water filling their boat. The real problem was that they didn't believe God cared. (Mark 4:38) Embrace this truth: God cares, and He's with you in the boat!

2. **Remember what you have.** When the widow was in debt and about to lose everything, the prophet Elisha asked her, "What do you have in your house?" (2 Kings 4:2) The solution to anything starts with thinking on what we already have, not what we don't have.

3. **Talk TO the problem; not ABOUT it.** The more you talk about it, the bigger it gets. The more you talk to it, the smaller it gets (Mark 11:23–24).

4. **Ditch the grasshopper mentality.** Numbers 13:33 says that the 10 spies brought back an evil report: ". . . we felt like grasshoppers, so that's what they thought too." That was the evil report. It's evil to think of yourself as smaller than the problem.

5. **The only giant in the land is *you*.** You don't have a giant problem. You are the giant, and you have a little problem. 1 John 4:4 says, "Greater is He that is in you, than he that is in the world." If the greatest One lives in you, that makes you pretty big!

6. **God is already on it.** Psalm 138:8 says that He will accomplish those things that concern you. No problem stands a chance against God's plan.

THINK IT AND SAY IT

The problem is not my problem. God is with me. He cares about me. His love is too great to let this thing defeat me. I have what I need to beat it.

I talk TO the problem, and it must obey me. I reject the grasshopper mentality. I am the giant in the land. I shall by all means go up and possess the land. The greater One lives in me, and that makes me greater than the problem, in Jesus' Name!

Day 33

"I Can't Shake My Past."

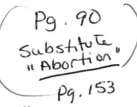

Today we fast from the thought that says, **"I can't shake my past."**

Often our past is what limits us and keeps us defeated.

LET'S CHANGE IT TODAY

1. **Meet the new you.** You truly are a new creation—if you are in Christ (2 Corinthians 5:17). The old has passed away. Your past is over!

2. **God will use your past.** Live in Romans 8:28. All things, including your past, work for your GOOD! While your past is over, God can still make it work to your advantage. Believe that.

3. **You are more than a conqueror.** (Romans 8:37) That means you are a conqueror over your past as well. It doesn't conquer you. You're the head and not the tail! See yourself that way, and your past loses its grip on you.

4. **You are *not guilty*.** No matter how guilty you were. You are now not guilty, because Jesus has washed all your sins away (Romans 8:34). That's how God sees you. Now, you can start seeing yourself that way.

5. **You *can* shake it off!** In Acts 28:5 Paul shook off the serpent. And you have the power to do so as well (Luke 10:19, Mark 16:18). Nothing can harm you anymore—not even your past mistakes or shortcomings. Shake it off by speaking to it!

6. **Have a funeral for regret.** Kiss regret good-bye. Have a burial service for whatever is nagging you (Hebrews 8:12). Take 20 seconds and pray this funeral prayer: "Lord, I thank you that this sin or mistake of my past is dead and gone. Into Your Hands I commit it. And I surrender these thoughts about it to You!"

And thus ends this funeral service!

THINK IT AND SAY IT

I am a new creation in Christ Jesus; and no matter how bad my past is, it's not only forgiven—it's washed away! I am more than a conqueror, and I will not be pushed around by memories or people from my past.

Because of the blood of Jesus, I am not guilty. I shake off my past. I declare it is over, and I expect God will turn my situation around for good in some miraculous way, in Jesus' Name!

Day 34

"I Feel Cursed."

Today we're fasting from the thought that says, **"I feel cursed."**

Many people feel cursed or unlucky when bad things happen, or when they seem to happen repeatedly. We can also feel like if a problem or disease runs in our family, it's bound to happen to us too. But it doesn't have to!

LET'S CHANGE IT TODAY

1. **The curse is already broken.** Galatians 3:13 says that Jesus redeemed us from the curse by becoming a curse for us, when He died on the cross. Identify with the finished work of the cross. Declare that the curse is broken and you are blessed, not cursed!

2. **You are of a new bloodline.** When you are born again, the blood of Jesus runs through your veins (2 Corinthians 5:17). Start expecting the blessing on His life, to be on your life. You are a joint heir with Jesus. You are His family, and His blessing runs in the family! (Romans 8:16–17)

3. **Adopt a covenant mind-set.** You are the seed of Abraham. Galatians 3:29 says, when you belong to Christ, you are Abraham's seed, and the blessings

that came to him will come to you. God made a covenant with Abraham to bless him in every way (Genesis 24:1). That promise is yours!

4. **Embrace the right version of yourself.** You can choose which identity you will live out: the one your family gave you, or the one God gave you. In Judges 11:1, history called Jephthah the son of a prostitute. BUT God called him a mighty man of valor. Choose God's calling over your life. Stop expecting the habits or problems of your family's past to be yours.

5. **Expect all the blessings because of Jesus.** Deuteronomy 28:2 says, "*All* these blessings will come upon you and overtake you." Blessings are no longer earned through our obedience but are given to you through Jesus Christ's obedience (Romans 5:17–19).

THINK IT AND SAY IT

I am redeemed! Jesus destroyed the curse 2000 years ago! I am of a new bloodline. The blood of Jesus runs through my veins. His blessing runs in the family, and I'm in His family.

I am covenant-minded. As the seed of Abraham, I expect His blessings in my life. I expect all the blessings to come upon me and overtake me, because I am in Christ Jesus. I refuse to accept what history calls me. I accept what God calls me, in Jesus' Name!

Day 35

"I'll Never Be Able to Change This Area of My Life."

Today we're fasting from the thought that says, **"I'll never be able to change this area of my life."**

We all have stubborn areas of our lives that won't seem to change—perhaps a habit, an attitude, our weight, or even a relationship. That ends today!

LET'S CHANGE IT TODAY

1. **Fast from wrong thinking!** You are doing that *now. When we change our thinking, we can change anything! As a man thinks, so is he (Proverbs 23:7).*

2. **Stop trying so hard.** Expect change to happen TO you, not BY you. Romans 12:2 says, "Be transformed by the renewing of your mind." Our part is to renew our mind by fasting from wrong thinking. God's part is to transform us. And He will! Expect!

3. **Give up on promising God that you will change.** Peace comes when you stop living by the promises YOU make to God; and start living by the promises HE makes to you. He will change you, as you renew your mind (Jeremiah 18:6).

4. **Think: fire and hammer.** Jeremiah 23:29 says, "Is not My Word like fire? And like a hammer which shatters a rock?" God's Word acts as both fire and a hammer. The Word does the work! Expect His Word to burn the stubborn area out of you with His fire or break it off of you with His hammer!

5. **Awaken to God's grace.** (Titus 2:12) His grace empowers us to change, to stop sinning, and to live godly lives. The river of grace is always flowing. Just step into it and receive!

6. **Refuse to give in to condemnation.** Condemnation keeps you bound to your present condition. When you realize Jesus doesn't condemn you, power comes to change you (John 8:11).

7. **Speak to the mountain that hasn't changed.** (Mark 11:23) Remember, whatever you bind on earth is bound in heaven. You have that kind of authority. Use your words to exercise your authority (Proverbs 18:21).

THINK IT AND SAY IT

I embrace the truth that as I renew my mind to the Word of God, He is transforming me. God's grace gives me the power to change. His Word is doing the work! As I speak God's Word and think God's Word, it is changing me.

I am free from condemnation, because I belong to Jesus Christ. That grace and freedom is changing me today, in Jesus' Name!

Day 36
Fasting from Excuses

Today we are simply fasting from **excuses.**

True success will never come to the person who makes excuses. We must eliminate excuse-making mentalities such as: "I can't do it without . . .", "I don't have enough resources . . .", "If I only had . . ."

Today we are going to eliminate excuse-making mentalities.

LET'S CHANGE IT TODAY

1. **Refuse to excuse mediocrity.** 1 Thessalonians 4:1 says, ". . . Excel still more . . ." Don't give in to the temptation to settle for where you are. Thank God for wherever you are at in life right now; and press forward for more of what He has for you (Philippians 3:13–14).

2. **Refuse to excuse lack and failure in your life.** Stop saying that you were born on the wrong side of the tracks, or you're limited by your upbringing. You may have been born on the wrong side of the tracks, but you're not bound to stay there. Cross the tracks now. Believe God will provide. Believe you are more than a conqueror (Romans 8:37).

3. **Refuse to excuse unforgiveness.** We sometimes think, "You just don't know what they did to me." But the truth is that God knows what we did to Him, and He still forgives us. Let it go.

4. **Refuse to excuse lack of support.** In John 5:7, the lame man said, "I have no man to help me." He used that as an excuse to remain in his condition for 38 years! Even if everyone lets us down, God will support us (Psalm 27:10).

5. **Redirect your effort and work.** It takes *effort* to come up with excuses. If we would redirect the same energy, and instead *look for a way* to succeed, doors would open. John 14:6 says that Jesus is the WAY. When tempted to make an excuse why you can't do something, ask Jesus to open the door that man can't close (Revelation 3:8).

6. **Get up on the roof!** Luke 5:18–20 says, "When they could not find a way to get in, they went up on the roof and lowered their friend . . . right in front of Jesus." They were relentless in finding a way to heal their friend. Refuse to accept that there is no way. Faith finds a way! Success will come.

THINK IT AND SAY IT

I make up my mind to stop making excuses. God has way more for me and I will not settle for less. I refuse to accept mediocrity. I refuse to accept my present condition as my final condition.

God will provide. God will support me. I refuse to blame others for my condition. I will not stay this way anymore. God will open doors for me that no one can close, in Jesus' Name!

Day 37

Fasting From Small Thinking

Today we're fasting from **small thinking.**

Most people probably wouldn't even consider small thinking to be a sin. But to *sin*, means *to miss the mark*. And if we are thinking any smaller than God intended, we are missing the mark. If we set up small and limited expectations of God or ourselves, that's all we'll get. The problem with that is God has so much more for us.

LET'S CHANGE IT TODAY

1. **Let go of a small god.** We were not created to worship a god invented in our mind. We were created to worship the God who made all things in the palm of His Hand! A small god needs us to pray louder so he can hear. A small god does not answer when we call (1 Kings 18:26–29). Little Baal couldn't answer, but our big God answered with fire!

2. **Think big.** Renew your mind to God's language. For example: "Ask for the nations" (Psalm 2); "Speak to the mountain" (Mark 11); "Your descendants shall be as numerous as the stars" (Genesis 15); "You shall possess the land" (Numbers 13). God uses BIG language and gives us BIG dreams.

3. **Ask for what you want, or settle for what you get.** Ephesians 3:20 says, "God is able to do exceeding abundantly beyond all that we can ask or think." Start asking and thinking the way God says to.

4. **Never stop dreaming and envisioning a better life.** In Acts 2:17 God says, "In the last days, I will pour out my Spirit upon all people. Your sons and daughters will prophesy. Your young men will see visions, and your old men will dream dreams."

5. **Don't be afraid of failure and disappointment.** If you shoot for the stars and end up on the moon, at least you've made progress. Let go of fear-based thoughts.

6. **Take your seat!** What do I mean? God has seated us with Jesus Christ in heavenly places. (Ephesians 2:6) We have been given divine authority and divine point of view. That's how we need to look at life. We are already positioned ABOVE our wildest dreams and expectations. So let's go get them!

THINK IT AND SAY IT

I let go of a small god and give up small thinking today! I agree with God's way of looking at things, and God's language. I decide to think bigger and bigger every day. I will dare to ask for the things God said I could ask for.

I accept the visions and dreams that the Holy Spirit wants to give me, and I let go of all fear-based, small thoughts. I have been given power, love, and a sound mind—to fulfill God's big visions and dreams for my life, in Jesus' Name!

Day 38

"I'm Stressed Out."

Today we're fasting from the thought that says, **"I'm stressed out."**

Stress is a powerful mind-set that we are going to dismantle. It is a collection of thoughts or fears that bear down on your mind until they penetrate you and control your emotions, your health, and your relationships.

LET'S CHANGE IT TODAY

1. **Know your enemy.** The real enemy is *thinking* that you have to get rid of the enemy. Psalm 23:5 says that He prepares a table (celebration) *in the presence of your enemies*. Begin to celebrate and praise God in the midst of the pressure, problem, or bad news. That's when it loses its power.

2. **The Prince of Peace lives in you!** (Colossians 1:27) Peace comes from the presence of God, not the absence of problems. Meditate on the fact that God's presence is in you and with you. Jesus said ". . . I am with you always . . ." (Matthew 28:20).

3. **Your treasure is greater than your trouble.** In 2 Corinthians 4:6–8, Paul said, "We are troubled on every side, but not stressed." Why? Because he knew

he had a treasure inside; the power to speak God's Word and change the situation.

4. **Be certain you are going to make it.** Uncertainty is a source of stress. Jesus had peace and even slept in the midst of a violent storm (Mark 4:35–39). How? Because He declared, "We are going to the other side." God's words create certainty and certainty eliminates stress!

5. **You're not *under* stress; you're *over* it!** You are seated with Christ in heavenly places—Ephesians 2:1-6. Live life from above—from God's perspective. You're above ONLY and not underneath (Deuteronomy 28:13). The battle is already won. Jesus did it all. Your fight is simply to believe that. That's when stress leaves.

THINK IT AND SAY IT

I am free from the power of stress. I don't have to get rid of all my problems to get rid of stress. I have a table in the presence of my enemies. They have NO power over me.

The Prince of Peace lives in me. I am certain I will make it. I am going to the other side. The battle is already won. Jesus did it all. My treasure is greater than my trouble, and I am above stress, and not underneath it, in Jesus' Name!

Day 39

"I Feel like I've Failed."

Today we're fasting from the thought that says, **"I feel like I've failed,"** or, **"I've failed in my relationship with God, in my faith, and in my life."**

The feeling of failure can be disheartening and depressing. It can keep us in a cycle of defeat.

LET'S CHANGE IT TODAY

1. **You have comeback DNA in you.** (Romans 8:11) Even in what seems like the worst situation, the same Spirit that raised Jesus from the dead lives in you. Expect your comeback! You have resurrection DNA in you!

2. **Fall-ing isn't fail-ing.** Proverbs 24:16 says a righteous man falls seven times, but he rises again! You are righteous in Christ (2 Corinthians 5:21). See yourself as someone who rises up. When you've fallen, you have the right to get back up.

3. **Jesus gets His prayers answered.** And He is praying for you, that your faith would not fail. Luke 22:32 tells us that Jesus said to Peter (and to *you*), "I have prayed for you, that your faith would not fail. *You are not going to fail.*

4. **Jesus is turning TO you, not FROM you!** In Luke 22:61, Jesus turned TO Peter after he denied Him. He didn't turn FROM him. You are accepted! This acceptance transformed Peter's life after he hit rock bottom. God accepts you, just like He accepted Peter, even when you've failed.

5. **Even when you're doing poorly, God will NOT FAIL you.** He's going to make sure you make it. Your relationship with Him was His idea, not yours. He will finish what He started (Philippians 1:6).

6. **In one moment, God can turn around years of apparent failure.** In Esther 9:1, God's people were about to be destroyed, but God suddenly delivered them. In only ONE DAY, the tables were turned, and God transformed certain defeat into total victory! If God could accomplish this for them, He will do it for you!

THINK IT & SAY IT

I have comeback DNA in me! It's my new nature to always rise, even when I've fallen. I have the blood-bought right to get back up when I've failed!

Jesus doesn't turn from me when I've fallen, He turns to me and prays for me. I cannot fail. He will not fail me. His love will never fail toward me. I am expecting God to turn my failures and frustrations around beginning today, in Jesus' Name!

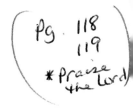

Day 40

"I'm Limited."

Today we're fasting from the thought that says, **"I'm limited."**

Perhaps you've felt limited by your past, your upbringing, or your pain. We all have something we think may limit us.

LET'S CHANGE IT TODAY

1. **God is able!** (Ephesians 3:20) He will do above and beyond all you can ask or think. He's not limited, and so neither are you, because you are made in His image.

2. **Meet Jephthah!** (Judges 11:1) His past told him that he was the son of a prostitute. *But God* told him he was a mighty warrior! Each one of us have conflicting voices telling us who we are. You must choose God's version of yourself, rather than people's version of you. Side with what God says about you.

3. **Leave the room.** The father of faith, Abraham, felt confined and limited by his inability to have a child with his wife Sarah. So God brought Abraham out of the house and told him to look UP and count the stars (Genesis 15:5). Whenever you feel limited, walk outside and *look up.* Look to God.

4. **You can only see stars when you're looking up!** Repeat step 3 above! Stop looking at the ceiling and start looking at the stars.

5. **Get in touch with your new spirit.** Your spirit is your vertical window, giving you the ability look up and see from God's point of view. Your flesh is your horizontal window, allowing you only to look around at your circumstance to look back at your past limitations. Open your vertical window and look up expecting God to do above and beyond all you can ask or think!

6. **Living beyond your wildest expectations and dreams starts with some wild expectations and dreams!** Dream big. Ask big. Expect big!

7. **Give God something to work with.** God builds His plan for your life when you think His thought, and dream His dreams. Then He does exceedingly abundantly above and beyond your highest thoughts and dreams! (Ephesians 3:20 Amplified Bible)

THINK IT AND SAY IT

I side with what God says about me today. I am a mighty warrior. I will not be defined or confined by my past. I refuse to be limited by my failure, mistakes, or the limitations others have put on me.

I leave the room where the ceiling is, and I look up. I look up, expecting God to do exceedingly abundantly above and beyond my highest hopes, thoughts, desires, and dreams!

Today I begin to see things from God's point of view—His Word—and I will decree His words, which will break through all limitations, in Jesus' Name!

Conclusion

Now that you've begun this revolution, *From the Inside Out,* let me encourage you with a few final thoughts:

1. **Expect things to get better!** Don't be discouraged if the miracle you need doesn't happen overnight. Fasting from Wrong Thinking is a process. It's the cocoon that awakens the power and beautiful destiny within you!

2. **Review regularly.** The devil will try to pull you back into wrong thinking. Whenever a negative thought comes back, speak to it with the thoughts and words in this book.

3. **Share your story!** Something that will keep you walking in victory is sharing how God has changed your life! Please send me your testimony at www.gregorydickow.com. It will inspire someone else to experience the freedom and change they've been longing for!

4. **Be a part of changing the world!** This is a movement born of God that changes people from the inside out! You can help bring this revolution to millions of others around the world by sowing a seed of any amount. Just log onto www.fastfromwrongthinking.com and click on *"Make a Donation."* Stand with me in getting

the word out about this life-changing Fast from Wrong Thinking. Remember, "As a man thinks within, so is he!" (Proverbs 23:7)

5. **Finally, don't ever forget this powerful truth: There is no stopping the man or woman who is set free from wrong thinking!**

Other Related Books by Gregory Dickow

- **The Power to Change Today**
- **Breaking the Power of Inferiority**
- **Conquering Your Flesh**
- **Taking Charge of Your Emotions**
- **Winning the Battle of the Mind**
- **Changed by Love**
- **30 Pearls of Pure Grace**
- **How to Fulfill God's Purpose for Your Life**

You can order these and many other life-changing materials by calling toll-free **1-888-849-5433.**

Also, prayerfully consider becoming a **Love Revolution Partner** with Pastor Gregory Dickow . . . changing the world one life at a time!

For more information about Gregory Dickow Ministries please visit **www.gregorydickow.org.**